Daily Life in ANCIENT GREECE

Don Nardo

raintree

Raintree is an imprint of Capstone Global Library Limited, a company incorporated in England and Wales having its registered office at 7 Pilgrim Street, London, EC4V 6LB – Registered company number: 6695582

www.raintreepublishers.co.uk
myorders@raintreepublishers.co.uk

Text © Capstone Global Library Limited 2015
Paperback edition first published in 2016
The moral rights of the proprietor have been asserted.

Edited by Clare Lewis
Designed by Philippa Jenkins
Original illustrations © Capstone Global Library Limited 2015
Illustrated by Roger@KJA-artists.com
Picture research by Jo Miller
Production by Helen McCreath
Originated by Capstone Global Library Ltd
Printed and bound in China

ISBN 978 1 406 28808 7 (hardback)
18 17 16 15 14
10 9 8 7 6 5 4 3 2 1

ISBN 978 1 406 28814 8 (paperback)
19 18 17 16 15
10 9 8 7 6 5 4 3 2 1

British Library Cataloguing in Publication Data
A full catalogue record for this book is available from the British Library.

Acknowledgements
We would like to thank the f[...] amy: charistoone-travel, 35,
dieKleinert/Bruce Emmett, 2[...]h Wind Picture Archives, 18, 37;
Corbis: National Geographic[...]o Bianchette, 38; Getty Images: De
Agostini, 34, 36, Print Collect[...]32; Newscom: akg-images, 5, 29, 30,
Manuel Cohen Photography,[...]bum, [...]bottom), Reuters/Mike Blake, 40;
Shutterstock: Anastasios71, [...]iguez, 31;SuperStock: DeAgostini, 26
Design Elements: Nova Deve[...]ock: imanolqs

We would like to thank Dr. A[...]ok.

Every effort has been made t[...] this book. Any omissions will be
rectified in subsequent printi[...]

CONTENTS

Some words are shown in bold, **like this**. You can find out what they mean by looking in the glossary.

"Future ages will wonder at us, as the present age wonders at us now!" These words were part of a public speech given in 431 **BC**, a little over 2,400 years ago. The speaker was Pericles, a government official in Athens, in south-central Greece. At the time, Athens was the largest and most influential Greek **city-state**. There were a couple of hundred of these states in what is now mainland Greece. Each had a central town surrounded by many villages and farms. Each city-state viewed itself as a separate, independent **nation**.

This map shows Greece in the fourth century BC, along with many areas the Greeks colonized across the Mediterranean world.

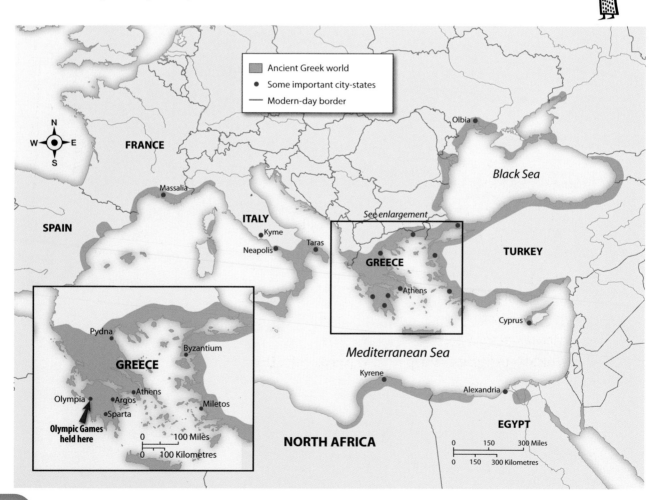

Ancient Greek world
● Some important city-states
— Modern-day border

N W E S

FRANCE

Olbia ●

Black Sea

Massalia ●

SPAIN

ITALY
Kyme ●
Neapolis ● Taras ●

See enlargement

GREECE

Athens ●

TURKEY

Cyprus ●

Mediterranean Sea

Pydna ●
Byzantium ●
GREECE
Kyrene ●
Olympia ● ● Argos ● Miletos
Athens ●
● Sparta
Olympic Games held here

Alexandria ●

EGYPT

NORTH AFRICA

0   100 Miles
0   100 Kilometres

0   150   300 Miles
0   150   300 Kilometres

Pericles also told his listeners *why* Athens would amaze later ages. First, he said, life in Athens was better than in other places. This was partly because it was the world's first **democracy**. In a democracy, people are free to choose their leaders. Some other Greek states had become democracies, but not all. And in Pericles' view, they had much to learn from the Greek way.

Modern historians call the period in which Pericles lived ancient Greece's Classical Age. They date it from about 500 to 323 BC. During those years, the Athenians created a democracy, along with some of the greatest art, **architecture** and literature of all time. These included the Parthenon temple on top of the **Acropolis**, the city's central, rocky hill.

People in later ages, especially modern times, saw these as great achievements. Many nations, including the United Kingdom, took up democracy as a form of government. They also copied Greek art, ideas and culture.

This picture shows Athens in the late fifth century BC, when it was at the height of its power.

The United Kingdom is a democracy. So much of everyday life is based on the idea of freedom. **Citizens** have certain rights, such as free speech and the ability to choose their leaders.

These ideas first appeared almost 2,500 years ago in Greece. There, in about 508 BC, the world's first democracy emerged in Athens.

Deciding their own destiny

Before Athens became a democracy, it was much like other ancient societies. Ordinary people played little or no part in ruling. They had no say in choosing their rulers, and there was nothing they could do if a ruler abused or cheated them.

Here, some members of the Athenian Council discuss the matters of the day.

Under democracy, Athenian citizens decided their own destiny. But the term *citizen* was defined narrowly. Only free adult males could vote or hold public office. Women were citizens, too, but they could not take part in government. Slaves were not citizens at all.

The Athenians who *could* vote, though, actually ran the country on a daily basis. For example, several thousand citizens attended regular meetings of the local law-making body – the **Assembly**. These gatherings took place in the open air on a hillside in the middle of the town. People clapped for speakers they liked and booed those they disliked. Eventually, they made up their minds and voted, and in this way the Assembly chose national leaders and made the laws that shaped everyday life.

TAKING TURNS AT CHANGING SOCIETY

All male Athenian citizens took turns serving on the Council. They thought of ways to make life better. The Council handed its ideas to the Assembly, which either adopted or rejected them. Almost every Athenian citizen, rich or poor, served on or worked for the Council at least once in his life. Many citizens served several times.

Athenian justice

Another aspect of democracy regularly affected the lives of many Athenians – the **justice** system. Each year, 6,000 citizens were chosen to serve as jurors. A jury for a single case could number 500 or more. Juries were so large to ensure fairness. It was clearly impossible to threaten or bribe hundreds of jurors to vote a certain way.

Athenian juries and court cases operated under strict rules. For example, there were no lawyers, so the **litigants** – the accuser and accused – made their own cases before the jury.

Athenians cast their votes to remove a corrupt or unpopular leader from office.

The Trial of Socrates

The most famous ancient Greek trial was that of Socrates. A well-known **philosopher**, or thinker, he encouraged people to always seek the truth. But some people found his ideas strange. So in **399** BC, they accused him of corrupting young people. It was not true, but the jury found him guilty and sentenced him to death.

This is why Euphiletus, a man accused of murder in about 390 BC, defended himself. However, Euphiletus did not actually write his own speech. Litigants who were not good with words were allowed to hire professional speechwriters. The well-respected writer Lysias wrote Euphiletus's speech.

When a person was found guilty of a minor offence, he usually paid a fine. More serious offences might result in the person losing his citizenship. This was considered a harsh punishment because he could no longer vote, serve on a jury or play other roles in governing the community. Plus, most people viewed losing citizenship as shameful. The worst crimes were punished by **exile**, or even execution.

Life in Sparta

Several other Greek states were impressed by Athens's democracy, so they adopted their own versions. Unfortunately, little is known about most of their governments and cultures. This is because the bulk of the surviving evidence for Greek life comes from Athens.

Like other Greek soldiers, Spartan fighters wore a chest protector made of several layers of linen and metal lower-leg protectors called greaves.

One major city-state where life was considerably different from Athens was Sparta, in southern Greece. The Spartans were old-fashioned and did not like change. They focused on the army. This put them at odds with the Athenians, who were adventurous, free-spirited and artistic.

There were relatively few free citizens in Sparta. These so-called Spartiates were soldiers. Under their control, most of society revolved around an extremely strict system of military training. It was known as the *agoge*. Boys had to leave home at the age of seven. They underwent brutal training and ate and slept in military barracks. The young men were not allowed to live with their families until the age of 30. This hard, heartless system produced the finest and most feared land army in Greece.

The Spartiates had many slaves to farm for and serve them. A few older Spartiates ran the government. The most powerful leaders were five men called ephors. They were elected by an assembly of soldiers. There were also two kings who ruled jointly. But their authority was limited to leading the army and overseeing religious affairs.

LEGAL MURDER

In Athens, laws against murder even banned masters from killing their slaves. In Sparta, by contrast, killing slaves was allowed. In fact, the *agoge* included **state-sanctioned** murder. At times, military trainees proved themselves by stalking and killing slaves.

In Classical times, many Greeks, including wealthy ones, lived in relatively simple homes with few or no luxuries. One reason for this was that Greece had warm weather most of the year. So most people spent more time outdoors than indoors.

Various kinds of houses

Farmers' huts in the countryside were often huddled together in small villages. These huts were built of stones, wood, clay bricks and thatch (bundled tree branches). A typical hut had one to three rooms. Country houses were somewhat bigger. The average one had a central courtyard open to the sky. They had five or more rooms.

The main difference between homes in the countryside and those in towns was that the townhouses were packed together along narrow, twisting streets. House fronts were most often plain and whitewashed.

 HOW DO WE KNOW?

The houses of Olynthus

One reason historians know how Greek houses looked is that some ancient writers described them. Also, the remains of a few of these buildings have survived. Among the best preserved are those at Olynthus, in northern Greece.

Many townhouses included a sitting room, workroom, kitchen and a few bedrooms. The poorest homes had no bathrooms, but some of the larger ones did. Some bathrooms had baths made of terracotta (baked clay). A few had toilets of the same material. Toilet waste and dirty bathwater flowed away to sewers, if a town had them. If it did not, waste water drained into a container called a cesspool dug beneath the house.

These surviving foundations of ancient Greek houses show archaeologists a great deal, including the layouts and sizes of the various rooms.

Food and drink

The kitchen was often the busiest place in the house. The women of the house, sometimes helped by slaves, spent several hours each day preparing and cooking food. Before the late 400s BC, most houses did not have proper kitchens. So some people cooked their food in wood- or charcoal-burning metal containers called braziers. Others cooked on stone-lined hearths. By the end of the 400s, many houses did have small kitchens, and most had hearths.

Olives were among the wide variety of crops grown in Greece. Here, farm workers pick olives and press them to make olive oil.

Most Greeks ate meat, such as pork, lamb, birds and deer, mainly during religious festivals. But fish was much more frequently eaten, sometimes every day. Most of the larger towns were near the sea, so fresh, cheap fish was easy to buy.

People also ate grains, fruits, vegetables and dairy products. Barley was the most common locally grown grain. Wheat did grow in Greece, but not very well in most areas. Large city-states like Athens **imported** it, particularly from Greek states on the Black Sea's shores. Among the Greeks' favourite fruits were grapes, figs, pomegranates, plums and olives. Popular vegetables included onions, mushrooms, lentils, lettuce and cucumbers. Cheese made from goats' milk and eggs were the most widely eaten dairy products.

The most popular drink in Greece was wine. People usually mixed it with water. This was done in a special pottery container called a *krater*.

PRESERVING FOOD

The ancient Greeks had no fridges, so preserving food was difficult. To make meat and fish last longer, people salted, dried or smoked them. Drying also worked with some fruits, as in the case of raisins (dried grapes). Pickling helped to preserve several sorts of vegetables, fruits and fish.

Household slaves and their duties

Much of the unskilled labour in ancient Greek homes was done by slaves. Unlike their owners, slaves were not citizens and had few or no rights under the law. The Greeks viewed slavery as a normal part of life. Indeed, even slaves saw slavery as natural. The proof is that many of the slaves who achieved freedom bought slaves of their own.

This slave is holding a box of jewellery for her mistress.

Most slaves in Greece were not actually Greek. People captured them in wars. Modern experts think that the average household had one to three slaves, but wealthier homes would have had more.

These slaves were both men and women. Female slaves made clothes, cooked, cleaned and looked after the children. Male household slaves did home repairs and helped with the shopping. They also oversaw the master's son at school.

Most household slaves in Athens were quite well treated. Laws protected them from serious abuse. But this was not the case everywhere. Spartan slaves, for example, were often mistreated, and some were even murdered.

SLAVES FOR SPARTA

Most Greeks thought it was wrong to enslave other Greeks. Sparta, however, openly broke this unwritten rule. Between about 735 and 715 BC, it conquered the neighbouring city-state of Messenia. The Spartans enslaved the Messenians, who became known as helots, and treated them brutally. This went on for over 300 years. Finally, in 371 BC the city-state of Thebes defeated the Spartan army. With the Thebans' aid, the Messenians regained their freedom.

Ancient Greek society was mainly run by men. The father usually made a household's rules, and all members of the family were expected to follow them. He would decide who the children were to marry when they became older.

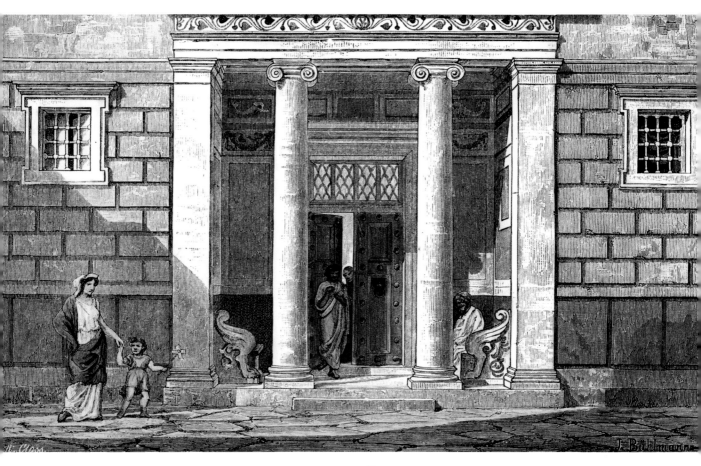

The rich decoration on this house shows that the owner was well-off. Most homeowners were men, who were also head of their families.

Women's place and duties

However, the man did not run the household on a daily basis. That was the woman's duty. She oversaw the children and servants, planned the meals and paid the bills. A story by the Athenian historian Xenophon shows that most men had confidence in their wives' abilities to carry out these tasks. The main character, a man, states, "My wife is perfectly capable of managing my household by herself."

The situation was different outside the home, however. In Athens and most other Greek states, women were second-class citizens who were mostly confined to their homes. Women *did* go out now and then. But it was seen as improper for a woman to appear in public by herself. Usually a male relative or servant went with her.

Women in Sparta

Female roles in Sparta were quite different. Due to the strict military training system there, most males were away from the home for long periods. So the woman not only managed the home, but also made and enforced the rules. In addition, Spartan women were not restricted to the home. They appeared in public whenever they wanted.

THE WOMEN'S QUARTERS

An Athenian man sometimes invited male guests to dine in his home. The household women were not allowed to attend, however. They retired to the "women's quarters". It was usually located in the back of the house or upstairs.

Marriage

Most Greek marriages were arranged. A young man's father and a young woman's father met and agreed the marriage would happen. The man and woman had no choice. Indeed, it was not unusual for them to barely know each other before their wedding.

An Athenian wedding party gathers outside a couple's new home. As they are today, ancient Greek weddings were festive occasions.

No precise descriptions of weddings in Athens and most other Greek states have survived. But modern historians have pieced together what would probably happen. In the afternoon of the wedding day, the bride's father held a feast for the families and invited guests. Towards the evening, everyone marched to the couple's new house. They sang a marriage hymn as they went. At the front door, they showered the bride with nuts and dried figs. Finally, the bride and groom disappeared inside.

Divorce

Not all ancient Greek marriages were successful. Divorces were not unusual, and the causes were similar to those seen today. Typical reasons were wanting to be with someone else, or one partner being cruel to the other.

In Athens, the divorce process was easier for a man. He simply told his wife to leave the house. She usually returned to her father's house, and that was that. A woman seeking a divorce first had to find a male relative sympathetic to her. The relative then went to a government official and asked him to grant her permission to divorce.

HOW DO WE KNOW?

Spartan marriages

Spartan couples got married in an extremely odd manner. Historians know this thanks to Plutarch, a Greek writer born in about AD 46. He claimed that the bride shaved her head bald and dressed as a man. Then the groom sneaked into her room "and carried her to bed". Afterwards, he sneaked back out.

This ancient Greek horse and rider was a children's toy. It was made of baked clay and painted by hand.

Children

The main reason for marriage in Greece was to produce children. Occasionally, however, parents did not want to keep a new child. If so, they left it outside to die. Some abandoned babies were rescued by childless couples.

As children grew, they played with toys similar to modern ones. Among them were balls, dolls, yo-yos and miniature wagons and chariots. Local craftsmen made most of these objects. But some children made their own, using whatever materials they could find.

MANY INFANT DEATHS

Child death rates in ancient Greece were huge compared to those of today. Modern experts think as many as 25 to 35 per cent of babies died in childbirth or early childhood. Compare this to a death rate of less than 1 per cent in the United Kingdom today. One cause was that people did not know about proper hygiene. Also, in ancient times medical knowledge was very basic.

Education

In Classical Athens, children's education started when they were seven or eight. Girls learned sewing, cooking and maybe some basic maths from their mothers. In Sparta, by contrast, girls were encouraged to be physically strong. They competed in running races, wrestled and threw the javelin. This, Plutarch wrote, gave them "a strong start in" building "strong bodies".

Meanwhile, Athenian boys went to private schools paid for mainly by parents. (The government paid for educating boys whose fathers had died in battle.) The instructors taught the boys reading and writing, poetry, dancing and playing sports.

The young Athenian women on the right are spinning wool into yarn. Those on the left use it to weave a garment on a loom. These were the types of jobs girls were expected to help with in the home.

WHAT JOBS WERE MOST COMMON IN GREECE?

Farming was by far the most common job in ancient Greece. Indeed, it was the main basis of the city-states' economies. Partly for this reason, people viewed farming as the most respectable profession.

In the distance, a Greek farmer ploughs his field to prepare for planting, while a shepherd tends to his farmer's animals.

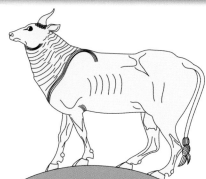

Tilling the soil

Greek farmers who grew barley and wheat planted them in October. They used simple wooden ploughs drawn by mules or oxen. The farmer steered the plough. A helper followed behind throwing the seeds. Harvesting and threshing (separating the grain from the stalks) took place in April or May. Mules did the threshing by trampling the grain on a stone floor.

Farmers picked grapes in September. They sold some to be eaten as they were. But they also crushed some by stomping on them with their bare feet. The juice was collected to make wine. From October to January, farmers harvested olives.

Many farmers also raised livestock, including sheep, goats and pigs. The sheep provided milk and meat, along with wool to make clothes. Among the other animals commonly raised on farms were cows, chickens and donkeys.

HOW DO WE KNOW?

Farming methods

Historians know about ancient Greek farming thanks to a few surviving Greek writings. *Works and Days* was a long poem written by a Greek farmer, Hesiod, in about 700 BC. Some experts also describe it as a sort of farmer's handbook. In it, Hesiod explains effective farming methods to his brother, Perses.

Other trades and jobs

Besides farming, many other trades and jobs were needed to make a Greek city-state operate smoothly. Plutarch mentioned carpenters, metal-smiths, stonemasons, sailors and wagon-makers.

Traders and potters were especially common and important. There were two general types of trader, or merchant. The first sold goods directly to shoppers in an **agora**, or marketplace. In operation most days, Greek agoras were open areas filled with merchants' booths, wagons or tents. Often the woman of a house sent a servant or slave to buy food there. Or she might go herself, along with a servant or male relative.

This elegant pottery container dates from about 470 BC.

HOW DO WE KNOW?

Potters' identities

Modern experts identify individual ancient Greek potters in various ways. In some cases, fortunately, potters signed their works. But many surviving Greek pots are unsigned. However, their makers can sometimes be recognized by the details of their styles.

The second type of trader supplied the merchants in the market with many of their goods. Most such suppliers were wealthy. They usually owned or rented the cargo ships that transported goods from foreign lands.

Potters were very important to society. This was because their goods were used by most Greeks. They created bowls, drinking cups, storage jars, vases and urns for dead people's ashes, to name only a few. Potters not only made these items, they also painted them. So they were truly gifted artists. During the Classical Age, most potters modelled wet clay on a flat wheel. They turned the wheel either by hand or by using a foot pedal. Then they baked the pots in a kiln.

Religious **rituals**, both public and private, played a major role in the lives of most Greeks. The belief was that the gods favoured those peoples who frequently worshipped them. Likewise, if someone disrespected the gods they might decide to punish the entire community.

Multiple gods

Like most other ancient peoples, the Greeks worshipped many gods. Each god oversaw a particular part of nature or human activity. The leader of the gods, Zeus, for instance, was a champion of justice. Zeus's brother Poseidon ruled the seas. And another brother, Hades, had charge of the Underworld. The ancient Greeks believed people's souls went to the Underworld after death.

A giant statue of Zeus, leader of the Greek gods, sat in its temple in Olympia.

HOME OF THE GODS

The earliest Greeks believed the gods lived at the top of Mount Olympus, in northern Greece. By the Classical Age, however, most people recognized this was only a story. They thought that the gods' home was somewhere in the sky.

The Greeks also saw the gods as **patron deities**. A divine patron favoured a particular city-state and protected it. Athens's patron was Athena, goddess of war and wisdom. Several of her myths were thought to represent real past events. One, for example, told how she became the city's protector by winning a contest between her and Poseidon.

The Athenians erected splendid temples in honour of Athena. The two most famous are the Parthenon and Erechtheum. Their ruins can still be seen at the top of the Acropolis today.

This 1512 painting shows Athena and Poseidon competing to become the patron god of Athens.

A farming family sacrifices a sheep at an altar. In the cities, family altars were usually located in or near the house's courtyard.

Common rituals of worship

The Greeks honoured gods and goddesses by carrying out daily, monthly or annual rituals for them. Of these ceremonies, prayer and **sacrifice** were the most common.

As people do today, an average Greek might pray at almost any time and in any place. Many Greeks prayed for help when something new was beginning, such as the start of a new farming season, trip or personal project. The Greeks usually prayed standing up with their hands raised palms upwards. The common custom was to pray aloud. In addition, there were public prayers in which hundreds or thousands of people prayed together. These occurred just before political meetings, athletic contests and even battles.

Sacrifice

People also prayed before or during sacrifices. Sacrifice consisted of an offering made to please a god. Most of the time people sacrificed at stone altars. Among the offerings made were liquids such as wine, milk and honey. Sacrificing animals, such as cows, goats, sheep and birds, was also widespread.

Other contact with the gods occurred through **oracles**. An oracle was a priestess who supposedly passed on messages from a god. People believed that some of the messages foretold future events.

The circular-shaped shrine of the Sanctuary of Athena at Delphi is near Apollo's temple, home of the famous oracle.

THE DELPHIC ORACLE

The best-known oracle in Greece was the priestess in the temple of Apollo at Delphi, in central Greece. People came from near and far to ask her questions. Often a visitor wanted to know how his village or city would fare in the near future. Both men and women also consulted the oracle for personal reasons. One visitor had difficulty in speaking clearly and wanted to know how he might overcome the problem. The priestess's answers were sometimes clear and uncomplicated. Other times they were in the form of a riddle and hard to understand.

The sacred Panathenaea

Other important religious customs in ancient Greece were religious festivals. Typically, these events celebrated annual holidays. Athens's biggest and most sacred festival was called the Panathenaea, meaning "all the Athenians". A very ancient ritual, the Panathenaea, held in July, got bigger every year. Apparently, it reached its height of size and splendour in 566 BC. At that point, it featured public feasts, large-scale sacrifices, and musical and athletic contests.

The highlight was a massive, colourful **procession** through the city streets. The marchers included elderly men; younger men on horseback; women and girls; children; soldiers in full armour; metics (Greeks from other states who lived and worked in Athens); freedmen (former slaves); and slaves.

The great procession wound its way through the city's streets and Agora. Then it climbed a large stairway to the top of the Acropolis. There, the marchers stopped near a large altar in an area between the Parthenon and Erechtheum temples.

In this section of the Parthenon frieze showing the Panathenaea, a man and boy fold the new robe made for Athena.

While everyone watched, someone presented Athena with a beautiful new robe. It had been made earlier in the year by some specially chosen young women. Worshippers draped the robe on a statue of the goddess in the Erechtheum. Then, hundreds of cows and sheep were sacrificed on the altar. Parts of the animals were burned for the gods, and the worshippers feasted on the rest.

Another section of the Parthenon frieze shows some of the young men who rode their horses in the great procession.

HOW DO WE KNOW?

The Parthenon's Frieze

Historians know who took part in the Panathenaea's great procession thanks to Athenian sculptors. They depicted the parade in a frieze, a long band of sculpted scenes, that decorated the Parthenon. Some of the frieze's surviving sections are now in the British Museum.

Ancient Greek life featured many different games and other leisure pastimes. Of these, the Greeks were especially fond of playing sports. This was partly because they felt it was important to be physically fit. Also, they loved contests. Greek men of all ages and social classes competed in games and contests of all kinds. Some were informal, like neighbourhood ball games. Others were on the community level and highly organized. Among these were contests to see who could produce the best music, poetry and plays.

The Olympics and other large-scale games

The Greeks particularly enjoyed athletic contests. This love of sports competition led to the creation of the Olympic Games, dedicated to Zeus. It is thought that the first games were held in 776 BC. They were then held every four years at Olympia, in southwestern Greece.

Two athletes compete in a game involving sticks and a small ball.

Athletic events like those of the Olympics were also held in this stadium at Delphi. Called the Pythian Games, they honoured the god Apollo.

Among the events were running races and throwing the discus and javelin. There were also combat events, including wrestling and boxing. In addition, Olympic contestants competed in chariot races.

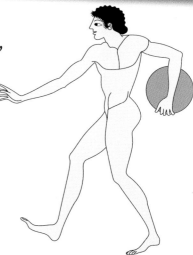

While the Olympics were going on, wars in Greece temporarily stopped. This was called the sacred Olympic Truce. All Greek states taking part in the games were expected to honour it. This ensured that athletes and spectators on their way to or from Olympia could travel safely.

THE WOMEN'S GAMES

Greek women were not allowed to compete in the Olympics. But they did have their own athletic contest – the Heraean Games. According to Pausanias, every four years, the female athletes had a running match. They "run with their hair let down," he wrote, "and their tunics rather above their knees."

Gyms

Large-scale games like the Olympics were not the only athletic contests. The Greeks held many smaller versions in individual city-states. Men trained for both kinds of games in gyms. Almost every Greek town had at least one gym.

Wrestling

Also common in Greek towns were places to wrestle. Wrestling was the Greeks' favourite sport. Boys and men of all ages frequently held friendly informal matches.

There were two styles of wrestling. The first was upright wresting. It was the only version allowed in the Olympics and other formal games. Each wrestler tried to throw the other to the ground.

A surviving vase painting shows two Greek wrestlers grappling. Two referees stand by, ready to punish a fighter who breaks the rules.

Men shared both drinks and ideas at symposiums.

The other style was ground wrestling, used in informal matches. It also started with the fighters standing. But after one threw the other, the match continued on the ground. Victory came when one person raised a hand to signal he had had enough.

Music and entertaining

The Greeks also loved music and dancing. Common instruments included flutes, harps, drums and the tambourine. There were many traditional dances, often with colourful names, such as "The Itch", "The Snort", and "Setting the World on Fire". Adult Greek men entertained friends at symposiums. These were drinking parties where men sang songs, told stories and played party games!

HOW DO WE KNOW?

Formal hunts

Those Greeks who could afford it took part in large-scale hunts. Men with hunting dogs, nets and other gear stalked hares, deer and other creatures through the countryside.

This reconstruction of an ancient Greek play shows the men of the chorus, standing on each side. They criticized or praised the main characters.

Going to the theatre

The Athenians invented the theatre. It is thought that a man called Thespis may have been the first actor and the person who wrote the world's first plays.

What is more certain is that a new Athenian public festival began in 534 BC. Plays were a regular part of it. The festival was called the City Dionysia. The name reflected that it honoured Dionysus, god of fertility and wine.

Each year Athenian playwrights competed to win awards for the best plays. They staged their plays in the Theatre of Dionysus, situated at the foot of the Acropolis. During the Classical Age, the Theatre of Dionysus could seat 14,000 people. Men, women, rich, and poor went to the theatre. The government paid for the tickets of the poorest people. The first plays of the festival began early in the morning, and the audience watched play after play until sunset.

The theatre at Epidaurus is the best-preserved ancient theatre in Greece. The modern Greeks still present plays there on a regular basis.

The spectators' seats rose up in front of the stage. It consisted of a semi-circle shaped stone floor and, behind it, was the *skene*, or "scene building". Its front wall served as a backdrop for the play's action. The actors put on their costumes and masks inside. Each mask represented a character, such as a king, messenger or young maiden. By changing masks, many parts could be played by just a few actors.

The most honoured playwright

Among the Classical Age's leading playwrights were Aeschylus, Sophocles and Euripides. Sophocles was the most successful, as he earned the top prize in the dramatic contests 18 times. Of the 123 plays he reportedly wrote, all but seven are lost.

The **legacy** of ancient Greek life turned out to be enormous. Many aspects of life in modern countries like the United Kingdom and the United States are based on Greek models.

Some of those influences are fairly obvious, such as democracy and trial by jury. Without them, people today would lack personal freedom and the ability to obtain justice. Another prominent Greek legacy is the Olympic Games. A group of sports fans revived it in 1896. That year the first modern Olympic contests were held in Greece to honour their place of origin.

The modern Olympic Games look very different but the idea came from the Games in ancient Greece.

GREEK ARCHITECTURE TODAY

Thousands of modern banks and government buildings feature stately rows of columns under triangular gables in the Greek style. This is very similar to ancient Greek temples, as seen in Athens's Parthenon.

Other ancient Greek cultural influences are less obvious. Most people see them every day without connecting to the Greeks. An example is when people watch a play, film or TV programme. The stages, scripts, actors, directors, costumes and even the awards shows were all invented long ago in Athens. Going to a gym is similar. While working out, few people think about the Greek origins of such places. And most people don't realize that history books, novels, philosophy and science also began in ancient Greece.

So much of the Greeks' culture lives on. In that sense, at least, ancient Greek life and society never died.

A day in the life of an ancient Greek child

My name is Agathe and I am **11** years old. I live in Athens with my family. In the morning, I awaken when the sun-god Helios begins to drive the chariot of the sun across the sky.

My first job is to collect water from the well in our courtyard and carry it in a pot to the kitchen. My father eats breakfast quickly and then leaves. He is a government worker and has important work to do. My little brother is eight. He started school last year and now he thinks he's very clever, reciting poetry and learning maths.

I don't go to school. But my mother has taught me to read and write a little, just as her mother taught her. Mainly, though, she says I must prepare for marriage. So she teaches me how to sew and cook and run a household. Father says I will marry in two years. He has a husband in mind for me. After that, I will be even busier. I hope I will be blessed with babies and, of course, I will have my own household to run.

In the late morning, I go with our slave to the agora to buy some groceries for dinner. It is always lively there and it's nice to catch up on the gossip but I return home as soon as my jobs are done. My place is in the home.

Our home is busier than usual at the moment. My mother had a baby last week, so people have been visiting and bringing gifts. The baby isn't named yet. Mother's last child died at only two weeks old, so my father is waiting to name this one.

Later in the afternoon, I beat and card wool so my mother can spin and weave it to make bedding. My mother prepares dinner of cheese, olives and bread dipped in wine. My father and brother return home. Father doesn't stay long. He is going out to a symposium at a friend's house. My brother and I manage to fit in a game of marbles before Helios and his chariot descend and we go to bed.

776 BC
The first Olympic Games is held at Olympia, in southwestern Greece

735–715 BC
In the First Messenian War, Sparta conquers its neighbour, Messenia, and enslaves its inhabitants

620 BC
An Athenian called Draco introduces a set of written laws

594 BC
The Athenians ask a widely trusted citizen called Solon to introduce government, court and social reforms. This proves to be a major step towards democracy.

566 BC
The Athenians reorganize the Panathenaea, their yearly religious festival honouring the goddess Athena, on a grand scale.

536–520 BC
The great athlete Milo, from the Greek state of Croton, wins the Olympic wrestling event five times

534 BC
The Athenians introduce a new public festival – the City Dionysia – which features the world's first plays

508 BC
The Athenians create the world's first democratic government

500–323 BC
The years of Greece's Classical Age as determined by modern experts. It includes the so-called golden age of Athenian culture during the 400s.

490 BC
A Persian army invades eastern Greece at Marathon, in Athenian territory. A much smaller Athenian army defeats and drives away the intruders.

480 BC
The Persians launch a major invasion of Greece. The major city-states of southern Greece work together and defeat the enemy in a series of battles.

464 BC

The Spartan helots rebel, but in a few years the Spartans crush the revolt

438 BC

The Athenians dedicate their new Parthenon temple, on top of the Acropolis, to their patron goddess Athena

431–404 BC

Athens and its allies fight Sparta and its own allies in the Peloponnesian War. Athens loses, but the conflict proves disastrous for all involved.

399 BC

The Athenian philosopher Socrates is falsely accused of corrupting young people. He is found guilty in court and sentenced to death.

371 BC

The city-state of Thebes decisively defeats the widely feared Spartan army, paving the way for the enslaved Messenians to regain their freedom.

338 BC

Philip II, king of the northern Greek kingdom of Macedonia, defeats Athens, Thebes and their allies. This allows Philip to control the big city-states of southern Greece.

336 BC

Philip is killed and his son, Alexander III, takes his place. In the years that follow, Alexander leads a united Greek army into Asia and brings the Persian Empire to its knees.

323 BC

Alexander, who will later be called "the Great", dies at the age of 32, possibly of alcohol poisoning. Modern historians mark this event as the end of Greece's Classical Age.

GLOSSARY

acropolis "high place of the city"; in ancient Greece, a town's central hill; the one in Athens is capitalized: Acropolis

AD short for *anno domini* - after the birth of Jesus Christ

agora marketplace in ancient Greece; the one in Athens is capitalized: Agora

architecture style of buildings

assembly in ancient Greece, a group of citizens who regularly met to choose leaders and make laws; the one in Athens is capitalized: Assembly

BC before the birth of Jesus Christ

citizen person who lives in and has rights given by a town or city

city-state in ancient Greece, a small nation made up of a central town surrounded by villages and farms

democracy form of government in which the people choose their own leaders and decide their own fate

exile banish a person from his or her city or nation

frieze decorative sculptured or painted band on a building

import bring into a country from another country

justice system of making sure laws are kept and of punishing criminals

legacy something left behind from people who came before

litigant in a court of law, the accuser or the accused

nation country

oracle message supposedly sent from a god; or the priestess who passed on the message; or the sacred site where she delivered it

patron deity god that favours and protects a certain city, nation or people

philosopher thinker, or someone who studies truth, knowledge and the meaning of life

procession religious parade

ritual set way of going through a religious ceremony

sacrifice offering made to a god or gods

state-sanctioned approved by the government

Books

Ancient Greece (100 Facts), Fiona MacDonald (Miles Kelly, 2009)

Ancient Greece (History Detective Investigates), Rachel Minay (Wayland, 2014)

Encyclopedia of Ancient Greece, Jane Chisholm, Lisa Miles and Struan Reid (Usborne, 2012)

What They Don't Tell You About Ancient Greeks, Robert Fowke (Wayland, 2013)

Websites

www.ancientgreece.co.uk/dailylife/home_set.html
This useful site from the British Museum provides information on Greek life based on scenes painted on vases and other pottery. Click on the "story", "explore" and "challenge" buttons to learn more.

www.bbc.co.uk/schools/primaryhistory/ancient_greeks/sea_and_ships
This site tells about ancient Greek ships and sailors. Click on the maps and photos to enlarge them. One shows a full-sized, working modern copy of a Greek ship.

www.olympic.org/ancient-olympic-games?tab=the-sports-events
The modern Olympic Movement presents this website on the ancient Olympics. Click on the tabs provided for lots of interesting information about the athletes, events and much more!

Places to visit

Ideally, of course, the best way to see ancient Greek sites, ruins and objects is by taking a trip to Greece. If that isn't possible, pay a visit to a museum.

The British Museum, London
www.britishmuseum.org
Visit the British Museum to see many objects from ancient Egypt.

World Museum, Liverpool
www.liverpoolmuseums.org.uk/wml/index.aspx
The World Museum in Liverpool has pottery and other objects from ancient Greece on display.

INDEX